Tao Passages

The Way Home

Dorien Israel

Library of Congress Catalog Card
Number 96-90769.

ISBN 1-879473-04-6

Willow Way
P.O. Box 3795
Reston, VA 20190

email: willowway1@aol.com

On the Cover

Soul's Journey, a 1980 watercolor painting by John Jerry-Anthony Parente, located in a private USA collection.

© John Jerry-Anthony Parente, 1980; the painting is reproduced here with the permission of the artist.

Widely exhibited, Parente's art can be found in many museums, colleges and religious institutions as well as in numerous private collections around the world. His work has a quiet radiance, a gentle reverence for all creation, and a "centeredness" that evokes a meditative response and spiritual power. Lyrical, sensuous, pulsing with movement and energy, yet possessing a deep inner stillness, Parente's watercolor paintings shimmer with layer upon layer of subtle glazes, revealing the transparency of the Divine in all. The relationship between art and spirituality is the focus of his work and life.

Those interested in his art may write: John Jerry-Anthony Parente, IC-RST. 28 President Street, New Rochelle, NY 10801.

These passages are dedicated to Mark Peterson, who has taught me the most important lesson left to learn in my life— how to die with dignity. I am grateful to Mark for so many things during the twenty years of fun and friendship we shared, but none more than this: I now know how to die.

I also dedicate these passages to Joan Peterson, his wife and my spiritual mother. I watched as Joan's love, will, and wisdom kept Mark with us on this planet longer than anyone thought possible. But in the end I saw her do the most loving thing of all—she let him go. To Joan and Mark who showed me the importance of the yang of living well and the yin of letting go. I love you both.

Acknowledgments

First I would like to thank my two sisters in spirit, Donna Hepburn and Jean Boston. Without their help and encouragement this work would not have been such a great joy to create.

I met Donna Hepburn in 1989 when my husband and I first moved to Asia. I recognized her immediately as someone I had been seeking for lifetimes. She, in turn, helped me recognize the true value of the writings I was receiving. Though great distances have separated us, our friendship has grown ever closer. She brings light into my life and the life of everyone she touches. She is an angelic being, tireless supporter, and my best friend.

Jean Boston started as a student in my meditation class but has since become both literary agent and true friend. She has helped navigate this material through the maze of a physical world I often find frustrating. Without her daily inspiration my life would be seriously diminished.

Thanks to Coral and Li, who are truly allowing the Tao to live through them, and are blazing the spiritual trail that always becomes the path that I, all too soon, will take as well.

In the most miraculous way, Donna Setzer came into my life bringing her gift of insight. She connected *Tao Passages* with the cover painting, "Soul's Journey," and kept the vision clear throughout the process.

Like any creative birth, this work needed the participation of men to help bring it into existence. Thanks to Bruce Boston, a professional writer and theologian, who questioned, critiqued, and balanced the process.

And, finally, thank you Gary Bietz, my husband and life-mate. When we first met in college in 1967, Gary was working toward his doctorate in Asian Studies and studying the original Chinese text of the *Tao Te Ching*. I believe our love affair has always been touched by the mystery and wisdom of Asia. This new version of the Tao feels like the culmination of a project started between us a lifetime ago. Thank you, Gary, for providing me with the firm foundation from which I am free to soar, for being my partner in the creation of our daughter Katetrine, so clearly a child of the Goddess, and for taking me to live in the Far East.

God bless us every one!

Tao Passages

The Way Home

To Deb,
I am so glad our
paths have crossed
here in Samui.
Thank you for sharing
your voice, your song
and the light you
shine.
Love, & laughter
Dorien
Samui
2018

Tao Passages One

The Tao is before conception
     and beyond comprehension,
     yet has it always been known.
Concepts may be used to communicate it,
     but they cannot contain it.

The Tao is eternal:
     birthed before heaven and earth,
     held between spirit and essence.

Defining creates the deception of separation
     within the Source,
     and words would make manifest
     what was once mysterious.

But, both mystery and manifestation
     arise from a similar root,
     and a Source can never be
     separated from itself.

Tao is the void of limitless potential
     out of which creation commences.

Dispense with your desires,
     renounce ambitions,
     deny all differences,
     abandon expectations,
     release distractions.
This helps clear the Way. ∞

Tao Passages Two

Separation at the source
    fragments wholeness.
If you see some things as beautiful,
    you condemn the others to being ugly.
If you see some things as good,
    by contrast other things appear bad.

Being and nonbeing complement each other;
Difficult and easy define each other;
Long and short depend on each other;
High and low bracket each other;
Before and after contrast each other;
Sound and silence speak to each other.

The Sage does not force the flow,
    nor does she divert its direction.
Teaching without intrusion,
    she lets things take their own course.

What arises she accepts;
    what disappears she lets go.
She has, but does not hold,
    acts, but does not exert;
Accomplishes without applause,
    finishes without fanfare.
What she produces
    is eternally fulfilling
    the part she has come to
    provide in the plan. ↕

Tao Passages Three

Seeking fame and fortune
    incites the People to corruption.
Striving for status and material substance
    stirs the People to compulsions.
Stimulating desires and appetites
    causes the People to grow greedy.

Therefore the Sage
    empties her head,
    so she is able to expand her heart;
    renounces her ambitions,
    so she is free to fulfill her aspirations;
    relinquishes her desires,
    so she might realize her dreams;
    relaxes her grasp,
    so she is able to embrace.

She is an enigma to those who pretend
    to know and those who profess
    to teach.

Let the living energy within you
    lead the Way. ❤

Tao Passages Four

Tao is the creative emptiness,
  from which springs the
  inexhaustible source of all supply.
Out of this mysterious womb
  wells up the essence of all existence,
  conception of all creation.

Soften sharp edges;
Untangle gnarled knots;
Disengage grinding gears;
Clean out old clutter.

It eternally evolves,
  yet it is fully formed.
A space without boundaries,
  a source without substance.
It fills us with inexhaustible potential
  and floods us with infinite possibilities.

Hidden within us,
  it is ever present. O

The Tao is indifferent;
     it regards all things as they are.
The Tao does not take sides;
     it is balanced between
     both good and evil.

The Sage takes things as they come.
She is not swayed by sentimentality,
     so she is free to form her own opinions.

Between heaven and earth
     lies the shape of things to come.
If you want to know what will be,
     then be all you know.
You cannot lose your Way
     for the Tao is a tether
     to which your future is tied.

Use it, it is inexhaustible;
Experience it, it is essential;
Live it, it is liberating.

Complexity creates confusion;
Surrender to the certainty
     of your own simplicity. +

Tao Passages Six

The Tao is the womb of the universe.
In its fertile void
    all things come to term.
Into its dissolving obscurity
    all things are put to rest.

Through the Tao
    you were brought into being.
Through the Tao
    you will be brought back.
Between infinite beginnings and eternal endings
    you are just meant to Be. ✿

The Tao is infinite, eternal;
     existing before birth,
     enduring beyond death.

If you seek to find yourself first,
     whatever you do will always last.
If you abandon your demands,
     your needs will always be met.
If you eliminate your excesses,
     you will be consummately fulfilled.
No longer hesitate
     to go the whole Way. ✽

Tao Passages Eight

The Tao is like water,
　　　　it flows endlessly from an unseen source.
Constant in its movement
　　　　it continually changes course.
Nourishing all things generously,
　　　　it takes no credit,
　　　　is never at a loss.
Beginning at its highest point,
　　　　it gathers itself at its lowest level.

In dwelling,
　　　　live close to the earth and stay grounded.
In thinking,
　　　　keep your mind open and thoughts high.
In meditating,
　　　　breathe into your being and expand
　　　　your own inspiration.
In speaking,
　　　　voice your truth and hold your tongue.
In relationships,
　　　　be generous and allow for growth.
In work,
　　　　make all things your labor of love.

Trust your divine nature;
　　　　disentangle from external demands.
The Tao is content to be itself,
　　　　neither competing, nor comparing.
In search of nothing,
　　　　it finds everything exactly as it should be. ≋

Filling to fullness is not as satisfying
        as being sufficient.
Sharpening excessively makes
        the instrument dull.
Those who hoard treasures
        become hostages of their own property.
Amass fame and fortune,
        establish success, exhibit pride—
        disaster will surely ensue.
This is only the natural cycle,
        bringing balance back into being.

This is the Way of Heaven:
        Do what you can,
        then quietly step back,
        and wait once more
        for the Way to be revealed. ➤

Can you blend your spirit with your body
    becoming one with well-being?
Can you coax your mind from conflict
    becoming one with all that is?
Can you ride your breath into your true nature
    becoming divinely inspired?

Can you encourage your insight,
    so heaven may be revealed
    through your vision?
Can you allow others to wander on their own path,
    even though you know the Way?
Can you deal with the most vital of matters
    by letting events take their own course?

Leading only,
    by quiet example,
Producing things,
    without possessing them,
Serving spirit,
    without striving.
This is the nature of the Tao. ✪

Tao Passages Eleven

We gather like spokes on a wheel,
    but it is the space we give one another
    that keeps us together.

We are like a vessel molded out of clay;
    but it is our open center
    that provides
    our real purpose.

Our bodies are like a house,
    a structure formed from substance,
    but it is the space within
    where spirit dwells.

The Tao is often disguised,
    even darkness and depression
    can clear a Way.
Gratefully accept what is given;
    learn to appreciate what is not. *

Tao Passages Twelve

Too much color blinds the eye.
Too many sounds deafen the ear.
Too many flavors dull the taste.
Too many thoughts fragment the mind.
Too many desires deplete the heart.

Become selective:
    allow senses to settle and be still,
    so awareness might be awakened.

Endless searching
    keeps you from
    valuing what you already have.
Constant moving
    keeps you from really being
    where you already are.
Observe the world,
    but do not confuse it with the Way. *

*E*xtremes endanger
        your balance.
Polarity pulls you
        off center.
Favor or failure,
        profit or loss,
        compliment or complaint—
Try as you may, if you
        pick up one end of the stick
        the other must follow.

Unconscious choices
        entangle you further
        upon the web of the world,
        risking your return home.

Stay still,
        the universe lies within you.
Have faith,
        the Way is without doubt.

Do only
        what is clearly yours to do.
Be careful
        with yourself, others, the earth.
Wake up:
        the Way is with you. *x*

Tao Passages Fourteen

Look! It cannot be seen,
      yet it is insightful.
Listen! It cannot be heard,
      yet it is constantly calling.
Grasped! It cannot be touched,
      still it stirs the soul.

Approached, you find no beginning.
Pursued, you find no path.
Followed, you find no conclusion.

Before beginnings,
      it remains endlessly present.
Between realities,
      it belies all existence.
Beyond comprehension,
      it knows the nature of all things.

Unbound—
      it enhances tradition,
      encourages transition,
      inspires transformation.

Its rising is the emanation of all lightness,
      its setting is the collapse of all darkness.
Whether you know it or not,
      you are already on the Way. ✿

Tao Passages Fifteen

One who is aligned with Tao
      is insightful, essential,
      provocative, resourceful,
Her essence is unfathomable,
      her demeanor ethereal.

The Sage is as
      conscious as one crossing a winter stream,
      courteous as an appreciative guest,
      changing as melting ice,
      simple as uncarved wood,
      clear as a newborn's eyes,
      peaceful as a monk in prayer.

Can you cultivate patience
      in the presence of chaos?
Can you wait for the silt of your mind to settle
      into the clarity of a worthy vision?
Can you resist interfering,
      and allow right action to arise by itself?
Can you remain at rest,
      even if the whole world passes you by?

Do you have enough courage
      to be free of convention,
      and enough conviction
      to follow the Tao? ø

Tao Passages Sixteen

Allow emptiness to envelop you.
Let peace pervade you.
Hold harmony in your heart.
Cultivate stillness.
Breathe inspiration.
Embrace serenity.
Become tranquillity.

These are not accomplished through your
        work, will, wishes, wants,
        desires, demands,
        prayers, or pleadings.
They are attained through trusting
        your divine nature.

The Way is not false;
        it will not lead you astray.
Refuse to follow it,
        and you will be wounded
        until you surrender...
                or die.

The Tao does not care;
        it will claim your allegiance either way.
But why leave this world before
        you have truly mastered living?

Everything that once flourishes dissolves
        again into the purity of its Source.
It is not a disgrace to die
        and be borne back to the One.

Do not cling so tightly to this world;
    you do not come from here.

Let yourself
        be amused, light-hearted.
Immerse yourself
        in the wonder of this world.
But be without expectations,
        prepared to be withdrawn
        at any moment.
This Way will not fail. ❧

Tao Passages Seventeen

Leave government to those who
    believe in being governed.
Let the People elect their politicians,
    nominate their parties and platforms,
    make their false pledges
    and empty promises.
One day they will awaken,
    concluding politics
    is not the Way.

Do not vote;
    instead devote yourself to the Tao.
Do not follow a leader;
    instead let yourself be led by the Tao.

If you want conflict and chaos,
    then elect more politicians.
If you want peace and sufficiency,
    then choose another Way. *

Tao Passages Eighteen

Justice and righteousness arise
  whenever the Tao is forgotten.
Cleverness and strategies abound
  whenever the Way is lost.
Obligation and duty are demanded
  whenever the natural harmony
  is disturbed.
Politicians and preachers are prominent,
  whenever a country has chosen
  to go the wrong Way. ↵

Tao Passages Nineteen

Renounce righteousness and
     give up morality,
     and The People will act ethically.
Discard legality and forsake justice,
     and The People will return to harmony.
Abandon profit and reject greed,
     and The People will generously give
     what they have
     and get what they need.

These, however, are worldly matters and
     as such, not vital to your welfare.
What lies within is essential.

Inspire integrity.
Keep to simplicity.
Hold to honesty.
Cultivate consciousness.
Temper desires.
Let go of demands.

These things will naturally rise to the surface,
     if the remainder are simply given away. ⁙

*H*alt your thoughts and there is
    nothing you will not know.
Thinking only confuses and complicates
    your natural capacity for clarity.
Stay still, be silent, and allow
    all answers to be revealed.

What is the distance that lies
    between true and false?
What real difference is there
    in success and failure?
They are but sides
    to the same coin,
Relative to one another,
    forged from the same family.

It is the mind that separates
    into desirable or detestable.
Do not be swayed by other's opinions;
    stand firm upon the foundation
    of your own experience.

The People are busy and impatient,
    self-absorbed and impulsive.
They believe constant activity
    actually brings accomplishment.
The People are reckless and heedless,
    gluttonous and greedy.
They believe the earth and
    her abundance are endless.

Do you believe you will not be
        held accountable for your actions?
Do you believe actions
        have no consequences?
Do you think what you are doing
        does not get noticed?

Without desires,
        you become unbound.
Without demands,
        you become sovereign.
 Owning nothing,
        you are free to simply be.
What other Way is there? ❀

Tao Passages Twenty-one

The Tao is intangible,
elusive, inscrutable.
It is with you always,
but without you the Tao is diminished.

Tao is without form,
so it must be sensed through intuition.
Tao is without image,
so it must be seen through insight.

The Tao is dark, empty, mysterious.

Do not be afraid;
those who follow become illuminated.
Do not doubt;
you already belong to the Tao.
Do not deny;
you are already on the Way. ✧

As you change, you become certain.
As you empty, you become fulfilled.
As you release, you become restored.

Having little you become light.
Having much you become burdened.
The burdened are unable to
        rise above their own limitation.

Therefore, the Master follows the Way
        so she may lead by example.
Since she does not show off,
        she is reflected accurately.
Since she does not boast,
        she is heard honestly.
Since she does not take credit,
        she is an addition to any situation.
Since she does not attack,
        she is invulnerable.

As you become one with the Way,
        the whole world will welcome you. ❂

Tao Passages Twenty-three

Nature speaks without words,
      yet who can ignore the changing winds?
If even heaven and earth are unable
      to make things endure, how can you?
Creating your own reality is not impossible;
      sustaining it is.

Be like the changing seasons,
      the passing clouds,
      the morning dew.

Do not doubt,
      your divine nature will deliver
      you to your ultimate destination.
Trust, and the Way
      will be entrusted to you.

Focus on the world
      and you will lose the Way.
Focus on the self
      and You will be lost forever.
Focus on the Tao
      and on the Way you will find your Self. ✿

Tao Passages Twenty-four

When you stand on tip-toe
        your balance is lost.
When you choose sides
        your stability is sacrificed.
When you stand in the spotlight too long
        you loose your vision.

If you defend your actions
        you attack your own credibility.
If you strive to get ahead,
        you have already lost the Way.

To one who is with the Tao,
        external achievements are meaningless;
        they will not endure.

Therefore, do not waste what precious time remains
        pursuing paths that lead
        away from where you are to BE.

The Tao is mysterious, formless, perfect;
>   birthed before heaven and earth.
Silent, serene, empty;
>   standing alone, infinite, eternal.
It is mother of all nature,
>   father of all time.

It pervades all things
>   perfecting them inside and outside,
>   purifying them at their source.

The Tao is great.
Heaven is great.
Earth is great.
Spirit is great.
This is the quartet of inner-chi.
The four great pillars
>   upon which all substance stands.

Revere them and be restored;
>   deny them and be destroyed.
Spirit, earth, and heaven
>   all follow the Tao.
The Tao follows its own nature.
Who are you to resist? ⊕

Tao Passages Twenty-six

Light is most appreciated
         after darkness.
Ascension comes readily
         after depression.

The Sage travels all her life
         without ever moving off center.
She is never distracted
         by the views of others.
She remains true
         to her own vision.

Why would the wise pretend
         to be other than they really are?
If you associate with fools for too long,
         you believe yourself to be foolish.
If you root around in darkness for too long,
         your eyes can easily
         become blinded by the light.

Alone, but not lonely.
Solitary, but not remote.
Singular, but not separate.

If you will remember the Way,
         who, what, where,
         and when follow effortlessly.
Why, however, will be forever withheld.
This is how you learn to trust the Way. ✿

Tao Passages Twenty-seven

One who walks this Way
    leaves no tracks;
One who speaks this truth
    voices no opinion;
One who travels this path
    cannot be misled.

A true teacher delivers no instructions.
The best defense is to let your guard down.
Real security rests in your Source.
The best protection is provided
    by a peaceful nature.

Thus the Sage knows no one needs to be saved,
    for no one can be lost along the Way.
Perfectly balanced between
    her creations and consumption,
    nothing is ever wasted on her.

What is a good man?
    He is but a bad man's hope.
What is a bad man?
    He is but a good man's fear.

All your knowledge is useless
    if you cannot recognize
    how easily roles and fortunes
    may be reversed.
You are your life's work.

Find yourself first,
    be yourself always;
This lesson lives
    at the heart of the Tao.

Tao Passages Twenty-eight

Engage the masculine,
    as you embody the feminine.
Provide a space inside yourself
    for creation to occur,
    and you will be eternally reborn.

Encourage the sun,
    as you engender the moon.
Become an accurate reflection
    for the whole world
    of the beautiful potential
    within human nature.

Inspire stillness
    as you employ activity.
Practice peace
    as you extend energy.
Share yourself endlessly
    as you keep close to your Source.

You will be known not by what you do,
    but what you refuse to do;
Not by what you possess,
    but by what you provide;
Not by how hard you exert,
    but by how much you extend.

Restoration is a gift given generously
    to anyone in repose.
Rest and allow the Tao
    to work its wonders through you.

Like a container of water
        resting within the enormity of the ocean,
So are you surrounded, as well as sourced
        by the consciousness of the Tao. *

Tao Passages Twenty-nine

If you look to the world for fulfillment
    you will find you have already failed.
The world is illusory;
    leave it alone,
    it is not the Way.

Why waste precious time,
    pursuing a purpose
    the world is powerless to provide.
    It is not the Way.

The world is fixed and constricting;
    it wants something from you.
The Tao is fluid and ever expanding;
    it is content just to let you be.

Sometimes you will advance;
    sometimes you will remain behind.
Some seasons you will attain your goal;
    some seasons you will drift without aim.
Sometimes you will be shown forgiveness;
    sometimes you will be fully to blame.
Some seasons will see you encouraged;
    some seasons you will find yourself drained.

Life is an endless ebb and flow.
Resist nothing;
    embrace everything.
Wait until the Tao asks you to dance,
    then let it lead the Way. ※

Tao Passages Thirty

Those who are in harmony with the Tao
        are without discord.
Enemies, arguments, differences, disputes
        depend upon which side you are standing.
Are you positive you know what may be wrong?

On this plane you can never promote good
        without providing for bad.
A concept can never come into creation without
        arousing its opposition.

You long for wholeness;
        yet the very nature of the world forever
        segregates,
        separates,
        and segments.

Can you lose control in order
        to consent to peace?
Can you let go of gravity in order
        to become light?

The meek shall inherit the earth
        and the earth shall show you the Way.
The meek are mild of spirit
        without malice aforethought.
The earth is your mother,
        abundant beyond belief
The Way is clear,
        without conflict.
Follow, and let it lead you Home. ↗

Tao Passages Thirty-one

Weapons are a sign of weakness,
    dangerous and destructive
    to the nature of all things.
The ignorant feel inadequate, act impulsively,
    arm and ready themselves for attack.
The Sage knows herself invulnerable,
    so she is reluctant to be provoked,
    and responds with equanimity.

Those in accord with the Tao recognize
    things are seldom as they seem.
One who appears to be foe,
    may in the end be our best friend,
    forcing us to face our greatest fears.

Those who are wise
    resort to weapons only when
    nothing else will work.
Those who see both sides clearly,
    know for every victor there is a vanquished;
    and in every triumph there is a tragedy.

Conquest comes at the cost of consciousness.
When you resort to weapons,
    the win will cost you the Way. ✠

Tao Passages Thirty-two

The essence and diversity
    of all creation are held within
    but a corner of the Tao.
There is nothing under heaven
    or upon earth that is without
    this elemental energy.

The Tao makes mountains high,
    oceans deep,
    and flowers open in their time.

When you experience your authentic nature,
    all of humanity is elevated;
    the promise of the prophecy
    is fulfilled from within.

It is time to exchange the guilt
    generated by the world
    for the grace given generously by God.

Guilt is literally the gravity
    by which the world hangs together.
Release yourself of this burden
    and become again light enough to leave. ❁

Tao Passages Thirty-three

Learning from others is education;
      knowing yourself is divine.
Mastering others is manipulation;
      subduing the self is sublime.

Control your appetite, appease your desires.
Demand no more than you deserve.
Preserve peace by being perfectly present.
Let go endlessly, so you may
      endure eternally.

Nothing that willingly surrenders
      is ever really lost.
Awaken to the wonder
      that waits for you within.
This is the dwelling place of the Tao. ✿

Tao Passages Thirty-four

The Vitality of Tao flows equally
        everywhere and through everything.
It withholds nothing of its own nature,
        so it is eternally fulfilled.

Though it is the Source to all substance,
        its essence can never be diminished.
Everything in existence
        arises from, returns to,
        and is dependent upon the Tao.

Because it makes no demands or claims,
        sometimes it is dismissed
        as small and insignificant.
Because it is the Source of all Heaven and Earth,
        sometimes it is revered
        as great and awesome.
The Tao is beyond both small and great
        beyond both none and many.
It is content to simply be as it is.

This is how Tao accomplishes all things.
Be who you are,
        do what you can,
        have what you need. *

Tao Passages Thirty-five

*B*e still, stay centered,
     and the world will lay itself at your feet.
What the world is starved for,
     you can supply by staying
     true to your Source.

Talk of the nourishment in the Tao,
     and the people complain it is too bland;
     it will not satisfy their voracious appetites.

Yet, the ignorant gorge themselves until
     their bodies become so burdensome
     their emaciated souls cannot support them.

Looked at, it develops no image.
Listened to, it makes no sense.
Tasted, it can never be consumed.
Embraced, it will never leave you empty.

No longer weigh yourself down,
     while you wait for the Way. ✢

Tao Passages Thirty-six

That which will soon be deflated
        has too long been full of itself.
That which will soon be impoverished
        has too long been privileged.
That which will soon be abandoned
        has too long been pursued.
This is the transitory nature of the world.

What the world once upheld
        will eventually be its downfall.
What the world once saw as successful
        will finally be seen as insane.

The Sage knows that real security
        cannot be found in savings,
        nor protection provided
        by taking up arms.
The true source of eternal power is found
        in connecting with the Tao.

The supple shall survive the strong.
The principled will outlast the privileged.
The meek shall inherit the earth,
        while the world stubbornly
        looks the other way. ▼

Tao Passages Thirty-seven

The Tao does nothing
    yet everything gets done
    in divine order and perfect timing.
Has winter ever forgotten to grow cold,
    or spring to bloom?
Do the tides ebb when they should flow,
    or the moon wax when it ought to wane?

Abandon your desires,
    retire your ambitions.
Align yourself with the nature of all things
    and receive your real inheritance.
Abide in the Tao;
    let it lead you home
    to a place beyond heaven. ❀

Tao Passages Thirty-eight

The eye cannot see itself,
    yet through it
    is the whole world revealed.
A fire cannot burn itself,
    yet it is capable
    of reducing the world to cinder.
A truly good man takes no notice of his goodness,
    so the effect of his actions is always good.

Fulfilling your true nature aligns
    you with the divine flow.
Who you truly are is always sufficient
    for the part you have come to play.

The vain live apart from the Tao
    so they feel separate.
Endlessly doing is their distraction,
    they believe it keeps them together
    but really it is all about to fall apart.

Sit still, be silent,
    allow your true nature to reveal itself.
Then whatever you do,
    will be worthy of who you really are.

When the Way is lost, goodness is initiated.
When goodness is lost, concern is revealed.
When concern is lost, justice is located.
When justice is lost, political correctness is left.

Political correctness is practiced when a country
        no longer knows what is right,
        so it is left standing on nothing
        but its principle.

The Sage sees beyond substance and into spirit,
        beyond knowledge and into nature,
        beyond sense and into essence.

Place your attention not on the beauty
        of the blossom,
        but the soundness of its root.
Remember all results come from
        the connection you share with the Source.

To foresee the future,
        remain fully in the present;
        this is where the Tao dwells. *

The Tao unifies all diversity,
Yet endows each aspect
  with its own unique essence.

The heavens are expanding.
The earth is grounding.
The spirit is uplifting.
The valley is sustaining.
The river is moving.

The expansion of heaven
    keeps you from being contracted.
The grounding of earth
    keeps you from being off balance.
The uplifting of spirit
    keeps you from being downhearted.
The sustenance of the valley
    keeps you from being depleted.
The movement of the river
    keeps you from being stagnant.
These embody the wholeness of Tao.

Each aspect fulfills its own divine nature
    through deedless doing,
    and selfless serving.
These are your truest teachers;
    honor their humility,
    learn from their legacy,
    trust their Way. ✿

The Tao's center is a spiral;
>   its dance is fluid, uplifting,
>   embracing you with energy,
>   moving you to your core.

Because the Tao is creative,
>   all things have their being.
When all things have been,
>   the Tao will be still.
This is the point where you
>   and the Tao may meet. ✸

When the wise hear Tao,
    they embrace it immediately.
When the average hear Tao,
    they entertain it occasionally.
When the ignorant hear Tao,
    they roar with laughter.
If the ignorant did not laugh,
    how would you know it to be the Tao?

The Way that enlightens
    is gained through depression.
The Way that advances
    appears clearly in retreat.
The Way that is simple
    is not always easy.
The Way of value
    cannot be bought.
The Way to creation
    is through chaos.

The deepest love
    is without attachment.
The greatest wisdom
    appears simplistic.
The sweetest sound
    is heard in silence.
The vastest space
    is found within.
The truest vision
    holds no views.

Seek the Tao;
      it is no-where to be found.
 Attempt to hold it;
      you grasp no-thing,
Yet by it are you
    shaped,
    supported,
    sustained,
    and sourced.
The Tao is with you all ways. ✫

The Tao gives birth
     to the One spirit.
The One cleaves itself
     into the duality of yin and yang.
Duality divides itself
     into the trinity of heaven,
     earth, and mankind.
From here all existence emerges.

The Tao birthed the One;
     that began the Two,
     who begat the Three,
     and became the Ten Thousand Things.
All things originate from
     and return to the eternal Tao.

Your lineage is ascended,
     your return is ensured.
There is nothing left to chance
     along the Way. ✿

Tao Passages Forty-three

The supple will survive the strong.
The simple will replace the complex.
The humble shall inherit the earth.
The world will receive the remainder.

Substance will surrender to spirit.
The Way will be known without knowledge.
Time and space will connect at their Source.
Vision will be restored through insight.

Action will be taken through acceptance.
Teachers will instruct through example.
Heaven will be restored to earth
        and balance brought back into Being. ✳

Which is more critical
　　　　to your well-being:
　　　　your health or your wealth?
Which is more vital
　　　　to your security:
　　　　your life or your living?
Which is more crucial
　　　　to your success:
　　　　adversity or advantage?

The more exclusive your love,
　　　　the greater your guarantee of grief.
The greater your greed,
　　　　the more you will have to give up.

Knowing what is enough is expanding.
Knowing how to stop is sufficient.
Knowing when to withdraw is wise.

The wise know the world is without value,
　　　　so this exchange will be easily made. ✦

Can perfection be evaluated?
Can justice be administered?
Can a winding path lead straight
        to your destination?
What is the difference
        between creation and chaos?
Where does a beginning end?

The Master manipulates nothing.
Secure in her Self,
        clear in her motives,
        refusing to react,
        content to let things be. ✳

When the world resides with the Tao,
    the earth rests in peace.
When the world rejects the Tao,
    the earth responds restlessly.

Wake up!
The world is moving the wrong Way.
Your will is free;
    choose again.
Do not interfere with the Tao,
    and your Way will be secure. ≋

Tao Passages Forty-seven

Without leaving home,
    you can experience the whole world.
Without looking out your window,
    the Ways of heaven can be revealed.

The more you travel in search of something,
    the farther you are from finding it.
The more you learn,
    the less you know.

Thus the Master
    knows without knowledge,
    sees without being shown,
    arrives without ever having left.

This Way brings you back to where you belong. ❏

The ways of the world
      insist on your increase.
The Way of the Tao
      rests on your release.
Little by little you let go;
      finally, you are free of attachment.
Doing nothing
      leaves nothing undone.

The world will be restored
      as you trust nature to take its course.
Keep all actions in alignment with
      the Way and worthy of
      who you really are. ♦

Tao Passages Forty-nine

The Sage has no mind of her own,
 responsive only to the moment.

So it is that she smiles
 on the good and the bad equally;
 is kind to the honest
 as well as the deceitful.
It is hard for her to discern the difference.

Be to all as a benevolent parent,
 gently guiding Wayward children
 back upon the path from which
 they have strayed.

Tao Passages Fifty

To live life fully, first see
　　　　it through the image of your own death.
The ignorant squander their time on things
　　　　that do not sustain the soul.
When you are really ready to embrace life,
　　　　hold onto the assurance
　　　　that too soon you will die.

Only after lying motionless
　　　　at the bottom of your depths
　　　　will you begin to perceive
　　　　the shallowness of your life.

As you break the surface of the water,
　　　　your first breaths
　　　　will be full of inspiration.
From this new vantage point,
　　　　you will be more inclined to enjoy
　　　　even the waves in your life.

Be as a knife cutting water:
　　　　immerse yourself in life,
　　　　and when it is time,
　　　　withdraw, leaving no trace. ✦

Tao Passages Fifty-one

*E*very aspect of creation
      is essential to the Tao.

Birthed into being by Tao,
      you are not greater
      than a single blade of grass,
      nor less vital to the success of the universe
      than a rising star.

To know your place in divine order
      brings constant harmony.
To forget your place in divine order
      brings endless misery.
Tao is contemptuous
      of those who are in conflict;
      compassionate to those in compliance.

Does this seem unjust?
When the baby bird falls from its nest
      can you see it from the cat's advantage?

This is the nature of truth.
This is the truth of your nature. ☆

Tao creates
all consciousness.
No matter how many images are reflected
there is only one mirror.
No matter how many ripples,
there is only one pond.
Be not deceived by diversity,
nor distracted by differences.
If you wish to witness the essence,
stay close to the Source.

Do not define your life
by the limitations of your senses.
When you open your mouth,
satisfy your senses,
ingest others' opinions,
your life force empties,
When you close your mouth,
quiet your senses,
keep your own counsel,
your life force fills.

Seeing the subtle is true insight.
Surrendering to the Source is real strength.
Being illuminated by the Way is brilliant. ✪

Tao Passages Fifty-three

Because I wish to be wise,
        I walk the Way of Tao.
My only fear is that I may stray.

This path appears straightforward,
        yet so many get
        sidetracked along the Way.

When the wealthy
        are unwilling to share
        the smallest portion of what they have,
When the officials
        take all of the credit
        while leaving the people in their debt,
When the people
        become numb to intolerable acts
        of unspeakable violence,
When the world
        becomes so warped
        it can no longer find the Way out,
This is certainly not the Tao.

If you wish, be in the world,
        but by all means,
        stay out of its way. ∽

Tao Passages Fifty-four

Your grasp upon the future
        is held securely within
        the roots of your past.

The Tao will become a true tradition;
        a gift given generously
        to each succeeding generation.

To transform the world,
        start with the self.
Cultivate integrity,
        and you will inspire it.
Your family
        will then reflect it.
Your community
        will then engender it.
Your country
        will then encourage it.
Your world
        will then experience it.

The Tao is contagious. ✽

Whoever is filled with the Tao
    becomes as a newborn child;
Although innocent and without defenses,
    he is immune to the attack of others.
Although fragile and delicate,
    his grasp is strong and without doubt.
Although powerless to provide for himself,
    he is nurtured without sacrifice
    from an endless source.
This is absolute affinity with Tao.

Knowing affinity provides fulfillment.
Knowing fulfillment reflects wholeness.
Knowing wholeness renders sovereignty.
Knowing sovereignty restores the soul.

Those who are in conflict with the Tao
    cannot be long sustained.

Therefore:
    refrain from rushing;
    do not coerce breath;
    conserve energy.

This is the Way of Life.
Is it the Way you live? ❀

Tao Passages Fifty-six

Those who know do not say.
Those who say do not know.

Close your mouth,
    still your senses,
    soften your sharpness,
    simplify your involvement,
    minimize your brilliance,
    humble your stature.
Bring yourself back to earth often,
    in order to remember your roots.

Lose the paradoxes,
    polarities, and
    opinions of others
Let yourself soar to new levels,
    so you may remember
    which Way you are going.

Although there are many paths,
    there is but One Way.
The world is going in a different direction,
    away from nature.

The Tao delivers you toward divinity
    while the world willfully denies it.

The more rules and regulations,
    the less resourceful the People become.
The more weapons and arms,
    the less peaceful the People become.
The more progressive and permissive,
    the less tolerant the People become.

Therefore the Sage
    embodies what she wishes to encourage,
    walks in the direction of her destination,
    and does not doubt the Way.

Tao Passages Fifty-eight

Governing with lightness
       allows the People to be uplifted.
Governing with heaviness
       keeps the People burdened.

Happiness is hidden within misery.
Misery is masked within happiness.
Wealth is wrapped around poverty.
Poverty is withheld through wealth.
The presence of one
       presents an opportunity for the other.

Who knows what turns the tides?
Who can say where the ebb ends
       and the flow begins?
Yet all are contained within the
       connection of the same sea.

Therefore the Sage is
       eternally vigilant,
       continuously conscious,
       ever present.

Balanced between either extremes,
       she never swims against
       the current conditions,
       nor finds herself caught
       between changing tides.
She has the stamina
       to ride whatever waves
       come up along the Way. ≋

Tao Passages Fifty-nine

When in true service
    to heaven and mankind,
    make certain you first center yourself.
Those too focused on serving
    lose sight of their own state of being.
Sacrifice of the Self
    has no place in service to others.

Instead, know that when ministering to another,
    it is always you who are the real recipient.
Thus humility is the sign
    of a true serving.

The Sage stays true to her source,
    rooted in reality,
    both feet firmly planted
    on the ground.
Leaving her hands free
    to reach for stars
    along the Way. ✶

Approach all activities on earth
in accordance with the Tao.
Be beyond both good and evil,
knowing that grasping for one
leaves an opening for the other to enter.

In the name of good,
much bad has been done.
But in rectifying many wrongs,
much good has been wrought.
If you wish to be further entangled on earth,
then engage in the pursuit of either one.

The Sage stays as still as possible,
until the Way presents itself clearly.
Then she aligns all her actions
with the intention of harmlessness
and moves in the direction
of higher consciousness.
This is the Way
freedom for all will be won. ✛

Nature is the most powerful
        presence on earth.
Because it is feminine,
        it flourishes.
Because it is secure,
        it allows all things to evolve
        and does not interfere.

The feminine overwhelms
        the masculine with patience.
She wields more power,
        because she yields more gracefully.
Because she can stay still,
        her energy is never wasted.
All of her movements
        are meaningful.

Be like a low-lying field
        full of potential and growth;
Open and receptive,
        attracting elevating energies.
Be ever constant and conscious
        to the changes that are coming. ✧

Tao is the source
        of all essence in the universe.
The virtuous know Tao
        and it becomes their provider.
The villainous deny Tao
        and it becomes their defender.
The Tao pays its respects to no one,
        allowing all to evolve accordingly.

What is it you believe you are pursuing?
Who are you trying to impress
        with grand gestures?
Do not attempt to disguise your intentions.
The Tao knows the difference.

Instead of presenting empty praise
        or expensive gifts,
        give of yourself;
Offer an authentic example of
        the Way to be.

Why have the wise treasured the Tao forever?
Because those who know the Way
        can never be lost;
And what has eternally been sought
        is about to finally be found. ❦

Tao Passages Sixty-three

Act without effort.
Accomplish without arrogance.
Heal without harming.
Expand what is limited.
Increase what is scarce.

Keep complexity
      from consuming you.
Traverse great divides by
      stepping beyond differences.
Do not deny what is
      in front of your eyes:
The most tangled knot
      can be undone one strand at a time.
The Tao achieves
      everything effortlessly.

The sage does not grasp
      beyond her reach,
      nor live beyond her means.
Her determination is not diminished
      by the difficulties encountered.
Because she is without expectations,
      she can never be disappointed.

Balanced between heaven and earth.
      suspended between spirit and substance,
She lives on a level that sustains the soul.

Earth gives her grounding and heaven
      holds somewhere for her to grow. ✢

Peace is most easily preserved.
Intention sets the best course.
Problems grow in proportion to their denial.
Energy follows thought.
Solitude keeps its own company.
Serenity is its own source.

Therefore the wise
        confront internal confusion,
        act on their own accord,
        consent to current conditions.

The tree never eats of its own fruit,
        but fulfills itself through feeding others.
So too the Sage releases her results,
        producing what naturally nourishes all.

Because she is wise,
        she can see that within every seed
        is contained the fruit fully formed.
Consistent in all endeavors,
        detached from all outcomes,
She allows all things in her life
        to develop in a natural Way. ★

Tao Passages Sixty-five

In the beginning of the Tao of time
    the earth was shrouded in
    darkness, mystery, secrecy.
The People were unprepared
    to receive revelations.
They believed they had fallen
    from the arms of God,
    and descended to the gravity of earth.

Now is the time of transformation,
    of prophecy, declaration, demonstration.
The Ageless Wisdom is available
    to anyone who truly wants to know.

Although you are alien to earth,
    your body was born here.
To restore balance back to the body
    return her to her natural resource.

When the body is brought into balance
    and the mind is at peace,
    perception becomes perfect.
This is the point
    at which to Be. ✪

*B*ecause the ocean trusts the Tao
     it lies below its tributaries.
Secure in its position
     it waits patiently for all waters
     to return to their natural source.

Earth is not your real home,
     but only a temporary port.
You have come here to
     experience and express,
     evolve and enjoy,
     evoke and endure.

Doubt nothing that comes from
     intuition.
Dismiss nothing that comes from
     imagination.
Deny nothing that comes from
     inspiration.

Whenever you are ready to awaken,
     the Way home awaits you.

Although there is only one Way,
      everyone is free to pursue her own path.
Regardless of the different directions taken,
      you will always be delivered back
      to the place you are destined to be.

What the Tao teaches is essential:
      simplicity,
      honesty,
      integrity.

Those who practice simplicity
      will find their way without difficulty.
Those who apply honesty
      will find their way without deception.
Those who embody integrity
      will find their way without deficiency.

Those who live in accordance with Tao
      find their Way without doubt. ✤

When you are with the Tao,
Who you are is in harmony
    with what you do,
Which is in concert with
    how you act.

Striving, competing, comparing
    are discordant to the Tao.
Be who you are.
Do what you love.
Have what you need.

This brings
    balance into being,
    wholeness into harmony,
    and faith into fulfillment.

Why would you want
    it to be any other Way? +

Tao Passages Sixty-nine

Because the Tao does not
        exclude anything in existence,
It is never in opposition
        to its own unity.
Free to experience all contradictions,
        it expands until it includes all aspects
        of its own infinite, evolving nature.

Therefore,
Contraction is naturally concluded
        by encouraging expansion.
Darkness is naturally diminished,
        by embracing light.
Resistance is naturally relieved,
        by unconditional acceptance.
Confusion is naturally corrected,
        by a commitment to clarity.
Conflict is naturally converted,
        by promoting peace.
Negativity is naturally neutralized,
        by a positive position.

There is no enemy,
        only unerring energy.
Do not attack what you are against;
        acknowledge, accept and allow it.
Do not deny what you dislike;
        experience and embrace it
        until it becomes transformed
        by the alchemy of your consciousness.

Within humanity
        there exists both
        harmony and unity.
It is your purpose to prove it. ✻

Although my words are simple
        and the Way is clear,
Few are fearless enough
        to follow the Tao.

For there is
        no glamour,
        no guru,
        no gospel,
        no grades,
        no graduation,
        no gain,
        no guilt.

When following the Way
        grace comes to you naturally.
Is there anything in nature
        that is graceless?

Because I am one with the Tao,
        many cannot see me;
Because I am one with the Tao
        most do not know me.

Although I may appear as others,
        there is a light within me
        that illuminates the Way. O

Recognizing ignorance is wise.
Ignoring ignorance is insane.
The insane are running the world;
     that is why it is so sick.
What ails the world is what
     you have come to cure.

To cure illness,
     start with the root it shares
     with illusion.
From this admission you may discover
     what part you play
     in perpetuating the pretense.

Do not look to the world
     for health,
     happiness,
     wholeness.
The world thrives on
     fear,
     guilt,
     judgment.

Search not for the Source
     outside of self;
     the Tao is not disguised.
Which Way are you looking?

Will you awaken
     from your nightmare of insanity?
Or will you continue to sleep
     your life away? ✻

Tao Passages Seventy-two

Are you aware of your awe?
Are you in touch with your innocence?
Are you in tune with your nature?
Are you in harmony with your heart?

Those who are awake live
        life in a state of perpetual amazement.
Because the Sage dwells in the higher dimensions
        she is content to keep a low profile.
The higher she rises,
        the more humble she becomes;
        this is how her balance is maintained.

The world is so weary of those who
        push and prod,
        demand and dominate,
        expect and exploit.
Will you choose this Way
        or that?

What really is there to do this day, but
        breathe in and breathe out.
Follow your own inspiration;
        the details of your day
        will be divinely arranged.

What if your true job
        was just to trust?
Could you curb your need to control,
        for a chance to really connect
        with your Source?
Stay close to your center,
        come straight from the heart.
Learn to live life in a new Way. ♥

The Way of the Tao
 is without doubt.
The ways of the world
 are without worth.
With the One lies simplicity,
 with the other lies duplicity.

The Tao does not effort,
 still everything is effected.
The Tao does not speak,
 still everything is communicated.
The Tao does not question,
 still everything is answered.
The Tao does not grasp,
 still everything is secured.

Though the Tao is always open,
 nothing ever escapes.
Though the Tao is always accessible,
 nothing is lost along the Way. *

*E*ach life on earth
  knows both beginning and end.
Like the cycle of the seasons
  your form forever changes too.

The opposite of death is not life,
  the opposite of death is birth,
  all of it is life.
Consciousness continues.

The unconscious live
  in a collective coma called denial.
Dwelling on your demise is unnecessary,
  but denying it prevents you from
  fully participating in life.
So fearful of the finality found in death,
  you forego the fulfillment found in living.

Do not be disturbed by death:
  it is only a natural deliverance
  into a different dimension;
Another perspective from which to view
  the wholeness of your life.
Life cannot really be appreciated,
  until death has been fully accepted.

Be aware of:
  all the roads untraveled,
  all the paths not taken,
  all the words unspoken,
  all the life left unlived.
This then is the purpose
  you are to pursue this lifetime.

Allow your breath
        to become your inspiration for life.
Exhaling, you let go
        of what no longer fulfills you.
Inhaling, you are again filled
        with the promise of perpetual renewal.
Holding onto or hoarding your breath
        only defeats your purpose.
Instead trust the eternal flow
        so you might be continually renewed.

The lessons you have come to learn
        are quite literal.
Live with the least amount of resistance
        to what is.
Be grateful and never take for granted
        all you have been given.
Make sure you never overlook
        the hope of what could be. ✿

*A*ll Ascendants are conduits
        through whom the Creator
        has chosen to come.
All Ascendants are light anchors
        lifting earth to her next level.
All Ascendants are preparing
        to open the Way.

But it is the women without menses,
        who will carry Christ
        consciousness to term.
It is the women who will provide
        the passage Way for peace
        to finally prevail on this planet.
It is not the virginal, but the vital,
        wise women who are the
        surrogates for the Second Coming.

Men are to support,
        securing the space
        for a new spirit to be delivered.
Unity between men and women will
        create conscious conception and
        provide the perfect place
        for heaven to evolve on earth.

Delivery of divinity
        does not have to be difficult.
What you do
        does effect the embryonic light
        that lives so tenuously within.

Therefore, do what any expectant mother would:
prepare, plan, pamper,
preserve your strength.
Proceed in peace,
progress in patience.
It is a time of turning
your total attention inward.

You are the Way,
the resurrection
will finally become a reality. ✚

Tao Passages Seventy-six

Your body is woven from
    the fabric of the Creator.
You are spirit born to substance,
    essence born of matter.

The body is beautiful beyond words,
    yet she is fed on positive phrases
    and nourished by elevated vibrations.
She is the transporter of your soul,
    and the vehicle of your psyche.
Through her are you moved in ways
    that transform your very existence.

Within each of your cells is contained
    the perfected memories of past millennia
    as well as the potential of all eternity.
Your body is the gatherer of wisdom and wonder
    that you will take with you
    to other worlds.
The greatest gift ever given to you
    is your body human.
Through all the forms ever taken by your spirit,
    never have you possessed
    a greater present.

The People's bodies are burdened by gluttony
    while their souls have become emaciated.
The People deny their body's need
    for spiritual sustenance,
    while their mind's appetite
    for material substances consumes them.

The body's needs are so simple
        in both design and desires.
Nourish her with whole foods;
        feed her with praise.
Move with her out of joy;
        exercise her right to be unrestricted.
Bathe her with clarifying water;
        shower her with love.

Your light body is beginning to be
        conceived out of your current consciousness.
This creation comes from your continued
        commitment to recognizing
        the resurrection as a reality.

This time when you exit earth
        you will not leave your body behind
        to be buried or burned,
        but will bring her back
        the same Way you came. ★

Tao Passages Seventy-seven

*T*he balance of nature
      is continually brought back into being.
This is the Way
      all things are meant to Be.
The Tao does not make distinctions,
      high or low, rich or poor,
      present or past.
It seeks only to share
      the abundance of its own nature,
      as it eternally restores earth's equilibrium.

Therefore those who follow the Tao know that
      all their efforts
         will be fully compensated,
      all their endeavors
         will be amply appreciated,
      all their accomplishments
         will be absolutely acknowledged—
Although this may occur in an unexpected Way.

This is a reminder,
      your real inheritance
      is held for you now
      in trust. ⁞

Tao Passages Seventy-eight

The Tao turns the tides
        and changes caterpillars into butterflies.
Do you truly believe that it has less magic,
        mystery, or meaning in store for you?

Pay attention to what within you
        is beginning to awaken.
The caterpillar can feel the essence
        of the butterfly,
        even before it begins to emerge.

Remember, butterflies are never
        born on the ground.
This type of total transformation occurs only after
        an arduous climb up the trunk of the tree
        and a perilous trip out
        onto the barest branch.
Risk is the cost
        of attaining anything of real value.

Create your own chrysalis of consciousness;
        a protective cocoon in which
        you realize yourself more wholly.
Dawning as a radiant light,
        awakening others in the same Way. ✸

The Way cannot be forced;
    forgiveness cannot be feigned;
    the future cannot be foreseen.

Let go of blame,
    and your body will become unburdened.
Shed hypocrisy,
    and your emotions will become unblocked.
Release judgment,
    and your mind will become unbiased.
Give up guilt,
    and your soul will become unbound.
Even anger can be held
    within a compassionate heart.

Always do what is right,
    rather than what is required.
Nature cannot be contained;
    creation needs no correction.
Blessings are but the natural result
    of being true to your Self.
Serenity always seeks its own Source
    and you are here as its living symbol. ☆

Conscious communities
        are coming together
        to provide a place for people
        to live in a new Way.
Awakened beings
        are beginning to gather in groups
        for the purpose of promoting wholeness
        in a harmonious Way.
Communities are being called
        by a deep intuitive longing
        to live in alignment.

All doing is done,
        and now it is being that has begun.
What you do
        is different from who you are.
 Simplicity will be
        chosen over complexity.
Peace will take
        precedence over power.
Presence will be
        more important than privilege.

Wherever possible, machinery that pollutes,
        and preempts people's own power
        will be abandoned.
Though there will be vehicles,
        essential movement will be made
        through alternative means.
While weapons will be available,
        after a while they will be put away
        and forgotten.
Although food will be simple,
        its nature will be wholly healing.

Rather than electricity,
        connection to the Source
        will provide the greatest power.
And it will be energy, not money,
        that becomes the major means of exchange.

In the future you will cry with disbelief
        at how ludicrous it was
        to steal and murder for money.
Paper is such a poor means of currency
        for there is no way it can conduct energy.

Those who live close to the land
        will cherish all aspects of life.
Death will become but a natural continuation
        of the creative process.
While birth will become the soul's commitment
        to the continuation of that process on earth.
To many this Way will appear primitive.
In reality, it is restorative in nature,
        and transformative in spirit.

This Cycle of Ascendancy is activated
        through the awareness of those
        who are awakening.
Peace resides in the present moment
        where mindfulness makes all matter one.
There shall soon be a collaboration of consciousness
        within a new community of humanity.

This is where divinity will dwell.
This is where the light will live.
This is where you will reside.
        This is the Way it will Be. ❖

Tao Passages Eighty-one

Words are worthless
    in their ability to awaken.
Yet, their vibration will remind you
    of why you have returned.
Sounds can communicate the Way
    that words never will.
It is not these syllables,
    but their sounds that
    stir the soul from its slumber.

It is not more knowledge,
    but wisdom that is needed now.
Wisdom comes from your attention.
What in the world
    are you attending to?

Do not follow fear.
Do not harbor hate.
Do not deny what you know.
Do not forget who you are.

There is a gateway that
    lies between the Way and the world.
It is a doorway that will deliver
    you into the next dimension.
It is not a dream, nor a fantasy,
    it is the fulfillment of the prophecy.

The passageway is perfectly proportioned
    with room enough to permit
    only the real you to pass.
What are you willing to let go of
    so you might lighten up?

What seems so essential to your nature
    that you would burden yourself
    by attempting to take it with you?

Let go of your need for long-term planning,
    surrender instead to the perfection
    of the present moment.
That which is saved for too long
    only tends to spoil.
Real security is found through an eternal Source
    that shares itself generously.

How long can you hedge your bets,
    hoping for heaven
    as you ensure yourself against hell?
"Give us this day our daily bread."
To say these words is nothing,
    but to mean them is everything.
They hold the means to an end
    of the old ways,
    and an invitation to initiate a new One.
This is a homecoming of the highest order.

There is only one time in which it is
    essential to awaken.
Now is the time,
    Here is the place,
        You are The Way.
            Welcome home. ✧

Afterword

For the past decade I have had a recurrent vision, a waking dream really, that continues to grow in detail and clarity each year. An envelope is delivered addressed to me, but not with my name on it. Instead what appears on the outside of the envelope is a sound vibration in symbolic form that resonates and so identifies me with who I really am.

As I open the envelope the light from within illuminates the entire room and it is this light that lets me know from whom this message comes. Inside there is an invitation asking me to attend the Third Millennium Transformational Gala for Gaia. Those are the words, no matter how much I wish they were not.

It is explained that those who had been present at the beginning of this experiment on earth are now being requested to return for the purpose of "reunion and resurrection." "In recognition of her millions of years of selfless service, Earth will be elevated from the status of a planet to that of a heavenly body."

Refusing this invitation, it says, is impossible "for the presence of each attendee is required in order to provide the perfect Passage Way necessary to complete this part of the evolutionary Plan."

This vision always ends the same way. I simply say — "I wouldn't miss it for the world."

Dorien Israel, 1996

About the Author

Dorien Israel has practiced and taught meditation and Qi Gong for many years in Hong Kong and Japan, as well as in the United States. In 1989 her first book, *Unbound: A Spiritual Guide to Mastery of the Material World* was published. In 1996 it was translated and released in Japan. The author currently resides in Thailand with her husband.

The author may be contacted via email at willowway1@aol.com or by writing to Willow Way, Box 3795, Reston, Virginia 20190.

Also available by the author—

UNBOUND
A Spiritual Guide to
Mastery of the Material World

by Dorien Israel

A resource that will transform your life and allow you to embark on the cycle of ascendancy. Written for those who are attempting to enhance their power to act on their own behalf and change their life.

UNBOUND provides detailed guidance to *the way home* through powerful exercises that will alter how you perceive reality. It takes you from where you are to a place where your spirit is free and your awareness is awakened.

Order from your local book store or from

Willow Way
P.O. Box 3795,
Reston, VA 20190

e-mail: willowway1@aol.com

_____

$15 paperback 188pp.
ISBN 1-879473-00-3

_____